WHY DOES CLIMATE CHANGE?

Investigate the Causes with Erica and Sven

LAURA ERTIMO & MARI AHOKOIVU

TRANSLATED BY
OWEN WITESMAN & MAARIT KAAIHUE

Sky Pony Press
New York

3

HOT DAY OR GREENHOUSE?

Does climate change mean that there will be a flood tomorrow or that next summer will be really hot? Not exactly. Weather and climate are slightly different things.

It would probably be good to lay out the basics.

Yeah—

first, climate...

...and then the change.

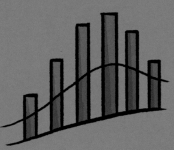

The climate is the big picture, the playing field that weather events run around on:
• How much does it rain during an ordinary year?
• Is there a rainy season or is it always dry or wet?
• Does it ever freeze during the winter? Is there a winter at all, or is the weather the same all year long?

You can learn about the **weather** by walking outside. You can predict the weather a couple of days in advance, up to maybe a couple of weeks. In places with highly variable weather, even a 10-day forecast is quite a gamble.

However, the **climate** is a more stable thing. For example, since trees don't run around chasing the rain, climate conditions have to repeat. All organisms rely on this for their survival.

The climate creates the foundation for vegetation, and vegetation supports animal life. The weather varies within the boundaries formed by the climate. But everything starts with the star called the **Sun**.

Weather can vary from day to day, and in different years, it can be a little different in the same seasons.
• Will it be rainy or clear tomorrow?
• Will it be below freezing or above during the winter holidays?
• Or do we even need to think about the weather, since it will always be warm and wet?

2008
2007
1999
2000
2001
2002
2003

If you're outside in nature, you can draw conclusions about the climate by looking around.
If you see a forest full of tall pine and fir trees, then you're in an area with cold winters.

Large expanses of sandy desert can tell you that it doesn't rain much where you are.

A high canopy of leaves echoing with the cries of parrots and monkeys indicate
a rain forest and a tropical climate.

THE WORLD'S MOODS

If the Earth was dry and there was no atmosphere, there would be no life. On the side facing the sun, it would be hot, and in the shadow, it would be cold. Places with mild temperatures would not exist. But the Earth has air and flowing water. Thank goodness! Different climate zones are the basis for life.

Different climates and vegetation dot the continents depending to how much sunlight they receive and how heat and humidity circulate. We bask in the Sun's rays at just the right distance, which gives us exactly the right amount of water in liquid form. Water is necessary for life, but snow, ice, and steam also play a role in climate patterns.

At the Equator, direct sunlight creates a lot of heat throughout the year.

You can't pile water. The water that flows in the sea has to be replaced by water from somewhere else. Sea currents even out temperature differences around the globe.

 The sun warms the surface of the sea in the tropics.

 Warm water currents flow toward the colder regions.

 The water releases its heat into the surrounding colder air.

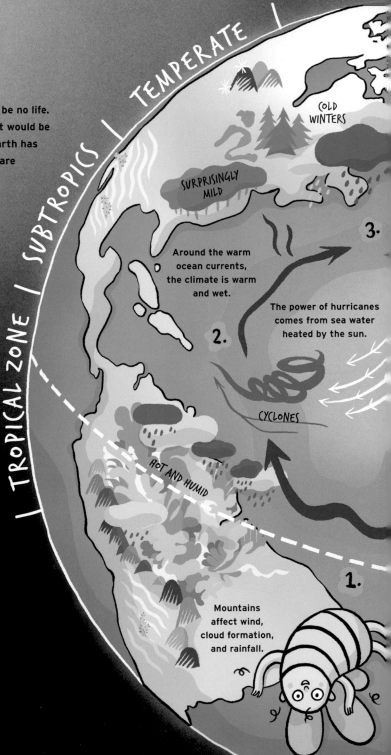

At the poles, the sun's rays always hit the Earth at a sharp angle, so there is less radiation.

TEMPERATE

SUBTROPICS

TROPICAL ZONE

COLD WINTERS

SURPRISINGLY MILD

Around the warm ocean currents, the climate is warm and wet.

The power of hurricanes comes from sea water heated by the sun.

3.

2.

CYCLONES

HOT AND HUMID

1.

Mountains affect wind, cloud formation, and rainfall.

COLD ZONE

Snow cover and sea ice reflect the sun's rays and cool the climate. The retreat of glaciers accelerates warming.

ICE

COLD

4.

ARCTIC CIRCLE

COLD WINTERS

TEMPERATE

Dark evergreen forests store heat until they are covered in a blanket of reflective, white snow.

 4. Some of the chilled water freezes. The remaining cold, salty water sinks to the bottom, where it returns to the Equator.

 5. Some of the cold water returns toward the tropics as a cold surface current.

This cycle will be disrupted if the polar glaciers melt and sea ice doesn't form.

The roots of plants influence the absorption and flow of water on land. In landscapes altered by humans, the risk of drought and flood often increases.

Because of the continents, warm sea water cannot circulate at the Equator.

TEMPERATE | SUBTROPICS | TROPICAL ZONE

5. Cold water does not release rain clouds or warmth onto land.

HOT AND DRY

DRY WINDS

The vegetation of rain forests contributes to rain cloud formation. Cutting down forests reduces rainfall.

Moving air masses like wind even out temperature differences. They may also transport moisture.

HOT AND HUMID

EQUATOR

but the laws of nature work the same as in the North!

In the South, ocean currents flow coun-terclockwise,

The larger climate pattern is also influenced by continents and oceans, and the ways they slowly change. In addition, the relationship of the Earth to the Sun varies slightly. The pace of change has usually been slow and steady, with epochs spanning millions of years and gradual shifts between ice ages and warm periods. Shorter fluctuations are associated with things like changes in sea currents and atmospheric composition.

As the climate warms, climatic and vegetation zones change shape. The climate map of the future will be new and unprecedented.

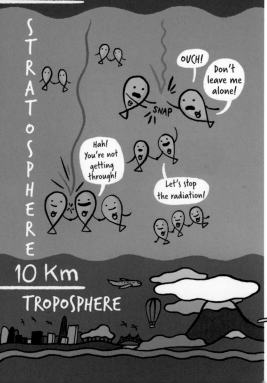

100 Km

MESOSPHERE

On the border between the atmosphere and space burn the aurora borealis. There, the air is very thin and gets thinner the farther from the ground you go.

Space particles colliding with the atmosphere flicker and flash as shooting stars.

50 km

STRATOSPHERE

OUCH!

Don't leave me alone!

SNAP

Hah! You're not getting through!

Let's stop the radiation!

10 Km

TROPOSPHERE

OUT OF THIN AIR!

The Earth is encased in a bubble of gas! It is invisible, odorless, and has magical powers. Well, not exactly magical, but Earth's atmosphere has amazing attributes that are the reasons we exist on the only living planet in the solar system.

Just think: if Earth was a ball three feet wide...

...the atmosphere around it would only be ¼ inch thick!

That's a pretty flimsy shield.

That's why it's so exciting!

The **stratosphere** repels the bombarding radiation of the Sun. On the surface of the Earth, ozone made from oxygen atoms is poisonous, but up high it offers excellent protection. Ultraviolet radiation from the Sun transforms normal oxygen into ozone, which protects life on Earth from that same radiation.

Closer to the ground is a layer, called the **troposphere**, where almost all the clouds stay. Here, the wind blows constantly and airplanes fly. Above this, air is much rarer, and you only have to go halfway into the troposphere before oxygen is in such short supply that it will make most people sick.

This book is about the warming of the troposphere.

The atmosphere is a gas mixture with different elements floating around in it—like nitrogen, oxygen, and argon.

Let's grab 2,600 gallons (10,000 liters) of atmosphere in a giant aquarium. Most of the mixture, 2,000 gallons (7,800 liters), would be nitrogen, followed by 550 gallons (2,100 liters) of oxygen. Argon and other gases would make up 25 gallons (96 liters) or about the size of a normal home aquarium. Carbon dioxide would only be 1 gallon (4 liters). A full 10,000 milk cartons of space, and carbon dioxide would only fill one normal 1-gallon carton! A goldfish bowl holds more than that!

Let's go, the milk is getting spoiled.

That's all dry air.

Although usually atmosphere also carries water and fine particles.

oh, that's such a small amount. Carbon dioxide must not matter much.

You're making a mountain out of a molehill.

That much carbon dioxide is like a fart in the wind.

$C + O + O = CO_2$

I'm famous!

Each carbon dioxide particle contains one carbon atom and two oxygen atoms.

Carbon dioxide is a transparent gas which is undetectable by human senses. It allows solar radiation through to the surface of the Earth but prevents radiation back into space—a little like the plastic windows of a greenhouse. Carbon dioxide is the most common greenhouse gas. This greenhouse effect is the reason we don't freeze like ice cubes on the night side of the Earth. The more greenhouse gases in the atmosphere, the less heat escapes and the warmer Earth's climate is.

Carbon dioxide is very **potent** in small amounts. This is why even people can affect their concentrations and aggravate the greenhouse effect.

GREETINGS FROM THE PAST

The Earth is 4.6 billion years old. All those zeroes mean that the history of the Earth has been full of more events and phases than we can count. The climate certainly hasn't always been the way it is now.

Rocks, glaciers, and layers in the ground allow us to study what conditions were present long before people began keeping records about the weather. What happened in the past helps us understand the warming that is happening now and its possible consequences.

4.6 billion years ago, Earth was formed

TIME

THE HURONIAN GLACIATION
In the distant past, there was an oxygen catastrophe during which some bacteria began to photosynthesize. An oxygen catastrophe doesn't mean a lack of oxygen but rather a release of oxygen into the atmosphere. For many bacteria, this was a terrible poison. It changed the **composition of the atmosphere** and the climate cooled. If an alien had flown by, he would have seen a planet-sized snowball in space!

LET'S PARTY LIKE IT'S HURONIAN GLACIATION

Trending!

Everything is connected!

2,400,000,000 YEARS AGO

WISH YOU CARBON PERI

359,000,000–299,000,0

THOSE WERE THE DAYS! IT TOOK HUNDREDS OF MILLIONS OF YEARS TO BUILD UP OXYGEN IN THE ATMOSPHERE!

THE CARBONIFEROUS PERIOD
The Carboniferous Period saw the growth of the world's first giant forests. The climate varied greatly. During cold periods, sea level fell, and during warm periods, it rose. Entire swamp forests were buried at the bottom of the rising seas and then squashed into coal, which has been preserved deep in the earth for 300 million years.

During the reign of the dinosaurs, huge amounts of the algae and tiny plankton living in the oceans sank to the sea floor. Over millions of years, this became oil.

PFFT!

HERE COMES THIS ONE!

THE LATE CRETACEOUS

The Cretaceous Period was warm. Then, when an enormous meteor crashed into the Earth, the climate and habitats changed rapidly. The Cretaceous ended with a mass extinction, which killed off countless creatures, including the dinosaurs. Some life did survive, though. Previously tiny mammals began to grow, differentiate, and fill the landscape. Birds remained as a living memorial to the dinosaurs.

HOLOCENE OR ANTHROPOCENE?

What should we call the current period? Is it the holocene, a short period between ice ages? Or is it anthropocene, the time of man, which will leave lasting marks in the rocks? What kind of change is happening now?

THE END OF THE CRETACEOUS ERA

OH NO!

66,000,000 YEARS AGO

SEE YOU AT HOLOCENE!

OR ANTHROPOCENE?

Even though we've only been measuring for a short time, researchers have precise information about the Earth's temperature over a very long period. We know that when people invented fossil fuels, a global disequilibrium began in nature. One disequilibrium is happening in the sky: the amount of carbon dioxide is rapidly increasing.

NOW!

11

A BROKEN RECYCLING SYSTEM

Carbon dioxide is supposed to be in the air, so what's the issue? The problem is that people mess up the carbon cycle by mixing slow-cycle ingredients into the fast carbon cycle. The speed of this change makes the warming dangerous.

Carbon is everywhere, including inside us. Because everything is recycled in nature, carbon moves from one place to another between the living and inanimate parts of nature.

The **fast carbon cycle** is a glimpse into the nature of life. We eat food and breathe oxygen. Using oxygen, our bodies release the energy in food for us to use. And then we breathe out the carbon dioxide. But how does the energy get into the food?

Plants absorb water from the ground and carbon dioxide from the air. In the chloroplasts of green plants, solar energy is photosynthesized into sweet packages called sugars. These sugars contain carbon, which comes from carbon dioxide. The energy contained in food comes from this photosynthesis. Plants recycle the exhaled breath of living creatures.

Carbon is also found in inanimate objects. In the **slow carbon cycle**, carbon travels between the Earth's crust, the sea, and the air over millions of years: it sinks into the depths of the Earth only to be ejected into the air, where it protects the Earth in the atmosphere before returning to become part of the sea and land again.

AND BACK UP!

HAHA

BUT WE ARE ESCAPING DOWN.

PLANKTON

(THERE ARE AN INSANE NUMBER OF THESE LITTLE GUYS!)

If organisms are buried deep underground when they die, the carbon they contain becomes fossilized. Fossil carbon escapes the fast carbon cycle—or at least it was supposed to, until...

FOSSIL SOILS

BOTTOM SEDIMENTS

Coal is burned in power plants for electricity and heat. Oil is burned in the engines of airplanes, cars, and ships.

MAKE ROOM!

But why does it seem like this recycling system is broken now?

Humans have sped up the journey of carbon from the **carbon reserves** of the slow cycle into carbon dioxide that actively influences the atmosphere. Fossil carbon should be released as the continental plates move over millions of years. Now, hydrocarbon compounds are being burned at high speed in internal combustion engines. So too much carbon dioxide is escaping too fast into the air.

The recycling system is out of balance because there are not enough recyclers for the carbon dioxide in the atmosphere. And to make it worse, the destruction of forests, swamps, prairies, and seagrass meadows **reduce carbon sequestration**. This is about a worldwide system. Atmospheric change alters vegetation, seas, and life in general.

Coal and oil are solar energy. So what if it's a little old and smelly!

People drain swamps and cut down forests. This leaves fewer areas to capture carbon.

But where is all that carbon dioxide supposed to go?

I found the problem!

There's more information here.

HEIGH-HO!

WHO WOKE ME UP?

...people discovered how to use fossil carbon compounds. The energy in oil and coal comes from exactly the same places as the energy in a carrot. But fossil fuels have had tens or even hundreds of millions of years to concentrate this energy.

WHAT'S BURNING?

So, there is too much carbon dioxide in the air that should be carbon in the ground. Where are the greenhouse gases coming from, and why on Earth are people burning oil and coal if it knocks nature out of balance?

Energy production contributes most to climate warming. People consume energy in countless ways. Natural landscapes also change as people alter the surface of the Earth for their own uses. Altering the environment for human use reduces carbon-absorbing vegetation and weakens the formation of carbon-fixing soil layers. **Carbon reserves** are emptied, and **carbon sinks** are weakened.

Who needs muscles?

Life isn't life without electricity!

ENERGY FOR MOVEMENT

Is your house warm? Use air conditioning!

ELECTRICITY AND THERMAL ENERGY

FUEL FO OTHER THI

Agriculture has its own special emissions. In nature, animals do not live in the same concentrations as domesticated animals on huge factory farms. This releases methane into the air, which is related to carbon dioxide and is a very potent greenhouse gas. In addition to carbon dioxide emissions, **industrial facilities** and **fields** also produce other gases that increase greenhouse gas effects.

CARBON DIOXIDE circulates in nature and plays the primary role in climate issues due to its high volume.

METHANE escapes into the air from cow farts and landfill gases. This is climate enemy number two.

NITROUS OXIDE, or laughing gas, comes mostly from fields. It is hundreds of times more potent than carbon dioxide as a greenhouse gas.

FLUORINATED GASES, for example, tetrafluoromethane, forces heat into the atmosphere thousands of times more efficiently than carbon dioxide and stays unchanged for up to 50,000 years.

ENERGY FOR THE INDUSTRIAL SECTOR

NOT NEEDED BUT STILL CREATED

RUNAWAY GAS

DUE TO OIL DRILLING

INDUSTRIAL PRODUCTION

BUY
BUY
BUY
SALE
SALE

More parking lots!

MORE SPACE FOR PEOPLE AND RAW MATERIALS FROM TREES

FOOD

NOT NEEDED BUT STILL CREATED

WASTE

THE UPSIDE-DOWN WORLD

The climate has already changed. Will we get away with it that easy? Getting comfortable in the illusion of normal is dangerous.

Man-made climate change is slow from the perspective of everyday life but fast for the climate. The Earth has become significantly warmer over the past hundred years, but usually people only compare the weather to the previous year.

At first, the effects of warming will be imperceptible, mostly affecting sensitive individuals and communities. Heat waves harm babies and the elderly. Warming, acidifying seawater destroys corals in the tropics. Arctic habitats are collapsing, but few people live on the changing tundra. The first mammal to go extinct because of climate change was an insignificant brown rat species on a small island in Australia.

Who cares?

It is foolish to think that climate change will only affect other people, not us. That we can shrug about rats and corals and continue business as usual.

The pace of change is uncertain, but the basic facts are clear. The water melting from glaciers will be enough to drown shorelines and coastal cities. Increasing temperatures may set off a vicious cycle in which the heat increases the warming. The consequences will range from floods to drought, crop losses to drinking water pollution.

The climate is everywhere, and climate change is having affects everywhere.

In the past, rapid climate change has been followed by the collapse of natural systems and gradual recovery in a new form. Our society rests on nature as we now know it, so protecting the environment is protecting people.

Sea level rise will not occur as a sudden, all-consuming tidal wave. People will have time to move to dry land, but the forests and cities won't. Their lives are measured in hundreds of years.

Some of the problems caused by climate change are already here, and some will crop up in the near future depending on our actions now. If we allow warming to accelerate, our circumstances will change at an accelerating rate. It is a choice to make big changes, and it is a choice to do nothing—there is no way to avoid this chain of events or to watch from the sidelines.

The good news: Even if the Earth's climate changes dramatically, life is unlikely to disappear completely from the planet. Even if some animals go extinct, the human species is quite resilient. Our extinction is not looming in the foreseeable future.

The bad news: Our way of life relies on fossil fuels. We have to break free from this addiction. We can face this as a shared challenge, or we can start fighting each other as we've done at so many other turning points in history. Fighting won't stop the warming, though.

WHAT IF WE DON'T GIVE UP?

The future will be different from the present, but can we influence how? It's time to dive into everyday climate change mitigation.

We challenge you to train and achieve your best CLIMATE CHANGE FIGHTING SHAPE!

Well, but we...

What do you mean?

THIS! No excuses. Time for action!

Home carbon dioxide emissions come from people surrounding themselves and doing their work with machines. So many products—necessary and unnecessary—are produced so far away that we barely even think about it anymore. However, producing food and consumer goods, and moving people and things, all consume energy. So do our homes, work, and hobbies. And the use of fossil energy warms the climate.

If you have the feeling that this isn't working anymore, you can start training for the future, too. You'll need information and you'll need willpower. **Ask yourself** and **find out**:

• What effects do my actions have? What do I need and what could I do without?

• The hardest question is: how can I change my necessary activities so they don't consume so much?

When you find answers to these questions, you'll be moving in the right direction and your changes will succeed. Something amazing might happen: **the future will become hopeful.**

EXERCISE #1: THE SMARTEST PIG BUILT HIS HOUSE OF WOOD

Building, heating, and providing water and sewer service for a house takes a lot of energy. Choosing a place and home to live in are some of the biggest decisions in life—including in terms of the climate. Wherever you end up living, you can fine-tune your emissions every day.

You can change the carbon footprint of your own life whether you live in the country or the city. The design of where people lives matters. For example:

In sparsely populated areas, everyday trips tend to be longer, and public transport is rare. Smooth urban public transit reduces emissions, but cities can also be full of people stuck alone in their cars idling in traffic.

Building with wood fixes carbon for the lifetime of the house, while concrete is a climate villain. When you build your own house, you can influence what materials are used. On the other hand, an apartment building can accommodate more people on the same land. Solution: wood apartment buildings!

Seen from the air, the green city of the future will be even better situated in its environment: green roofs and wall gardens, water permeable and mentally invigorating green areas will become a living blanket for cities. Plants:

- purify the air
- fix carbon
- equalize temperatures
- mitigate floods

Everything you need will be close by. Even food will be produced in the city.

Energy will be produced locally. Walking and biking will be easy.

People are born every day—are we going to run out of space? But lots of people can fit into cities. And in **green** cities, everyone wins, even wild animals. (During the time this book was being written, a wolf, a wolverine, sea eagles, eagle owls, and ringed seals were seen in Helsinki...)

But kids don't decide where they live or design cities.

Until they grow up.

But I think you can probably do stuff at home, too.

Let's make a list!

1. Heating homes in the winter consumes a lot of energy. Let's turn down the heat by a couple of degrees and put on wool socks when it's cold. Geothermal heat and heat pumps, along with proper insulation, take care of the heating problem using technology.

2. Where does electricity come from? Household appliances and electronics use electricity. Take a look at your energy contract: ecological electricity is produced using wind and solar power. Solar panels on your roof can produce true local electricity. Light your life with LED lamps and choose durable, energy-efficient electrical appliances.

3. Even water matters! Water purification and heating take a lot of energy, and so does wastewater treatment (but it's even worse if the waste ends up in the sea without being purified). So, the less time you spend in the shower and the less water you use, the better.

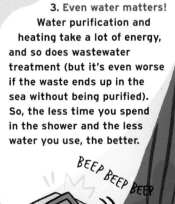

BEEP BEEP BEEP

EXERCISE #2: THE PLANETARY DIET

So, does it really matter what you eat—spaghetti and meatballs or a glass of milk? Yes. Dietary choices can do wonders for your carbon footprint.

This food thing is a real jungle, but at least vegetarian food seems to be a winner.

But what about my dreams of being a professional cyclist?

Will my big, muscled thighs shrink to nothing if I start gnawing on carrots?

Let's Google it!

Triathlon!

Ultra-running!

Body-building!

Thai boxing!

At the top of all the hardest sports, you can find athletes who don't eat meat!

A hamburger a day? The difference between ground beef and a tofu burger is that one is beans and the other is dead cows. Both are sources of protein. The impact on the climate is completely different, though.

ONE GROUND BEEF PATTY (75 g)

2820 kg CO₂e

BEEF EVERY DAY FOR A YEAR

equivalent to flying from Helsinki to Los Angeles

452 kg CO₂e

BEEF ONCE A WEEK, OTHER DAYS TOFU

equivalent to one flight from Helsinki to Nice

ONE TOFU BURGER (100G)

58 kg CO₂e

TOFU EVERY DAY FOR A YEAR

equivalent to one round trip flight to Tallinn, Estonia

SOURCE: BBC.COM, CLIMATE CHANGE FOOD CALCULATOR

On many farms, animals are fed soy produced in South America. There, they cut down rain forests to make space for soy bean fields. When you leave out the meat production and eat the soy yourself, for example as tofu, less field space is needed, and no methane emissions are caused.

Vegetarian food: bigger portions, smaller carbon footprint.

Why does she get a bigger burger?

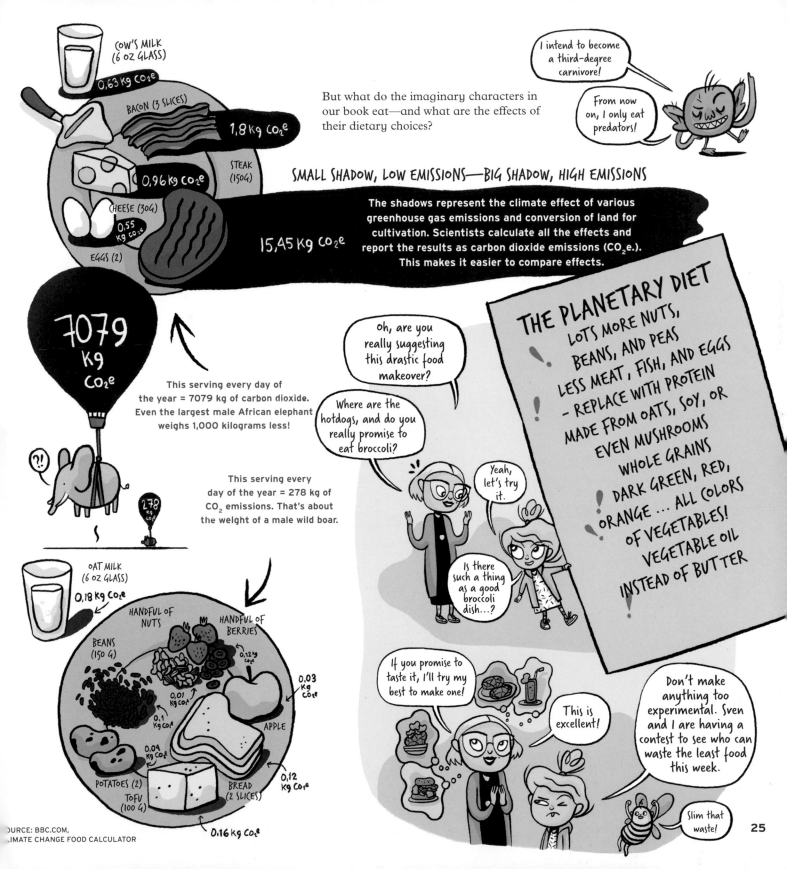

EXERCISE #3:
AN EMBARRASSMENT OF RICHES

How is it possible that 50 years ago we survived without mobile phones, toys from fast food kids' meals, and special shoes for every road surface and weather condition? And what about battery-operated hand soap dispensers, leaf blowers, T-shirts that only last a week, and electric nose hair clippers? Everything is advertised as a precision instrument.

There are many problems involved in the **manufacture**, **transportation**, and **marketing** of consumer goods, as well as their **disposal** when they're no longer needed. In terms of the climate, there isn't much to ponder about the shopper's paradise we've created: making new goods always consumes natural resources and produces emissions.

Write this second:

CAN YOU FIND IT USED?

Next to that, we could put:

3. ALSO MAKE SURE YOUR OWN STUFF GETS REUSED

And then last, we could write:

4. MAKE IT YOURSELF.

Not buying is the best decision for the climate!

When buying something new, it's especially important to be alert. Can you determine the circumstances under which the item was made? Some products have detailed labels but most don't. You can always ask the merchant about the production methods, but be prepared for them to scratch their heads. The more people ask about manufacturing, the more producers will have to pay attention to it.

The best solutions to this problem are reducing, reusing, recycling, and being smart about new purchases. However, there's no need to turn back the clock—better to invent new ways of taking care of people's well-being and nature at the same time.

Outside of the shopping mall, you can consume almost **without noticing**. For example, you might think that your sports hobbies only take muscle energy. However, many hobbies require a big pile of equipment and special buildings with heating and cooling.

Even using a mobile phone can involve big emissions. HD video streaming requires a lot of server power, and that means energy consumption. Globally, emissions from telecommunications and data traffic is on par with aviation, so you can even make climate choices about your entertainment.

HAHAHA! Used clothes! old phone! You must be poor.

How embarrassing!

Listen, gremlin, we're rewriting the rules of embarrassment.

Now, conspicuous consumption is embarrassing.

What if you gave all that racket and farting a rest?

That would be wild. Want to join our climate action team?

EXERCISE #4: **REAL EXERCISE**

An individual person can cause his or her greatest single carbon dioxide emission by flying in an airplane. However, most transportation emissions happen on the road. Is that a paradox? Maybe we just have to think about moving in a new way.

Migratory birds can tell you that **flying** is a great way to go far fast. But there is also a big, coal-black secret associated with airplanes, because their emissions end up directly in the stratosphere. There, the effect of carbon dioxide is much greater than closer to the ground.

You can also travel a long way **on land.** Trains are clear winners in long-distance emissions comparisons, with a trip from Helsinki, Finland, to Paris, France, producing only about 6kg of carbon dioxide emissions.

Everyday driving, both to transport people and goods using internal combustion engines, produces the lion's share of all transportation greenhouse gases. Even though flying takes up a terrible amount of energy, much more time is spent in cars, so the total emissions are larger. That means that every trip you take on public transit—or even better, under your own muscle power—is a good deed for the climate.

The average Finn's carbon footprint is 10,300 kg CO_2e/year including living, eating, and moving. The average American's, by contrast, is 16 tons CO_2e/year.
SOURCE: SITRA & NATURE.ORG

Relax on a staycation close to home

...or go on a train adventure!

Take a fitness vacation by bike,

TRACK 2

Here's how you can cause the same emissions either by living one year of life in Finland or flying for about two days.

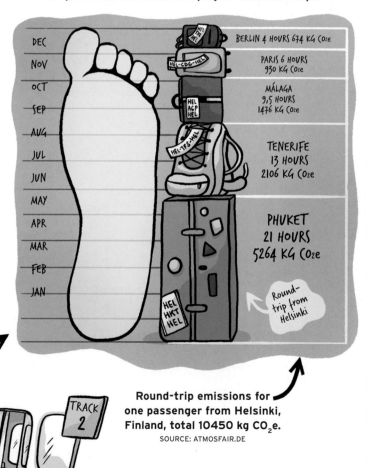

DEC
NOV
OCT
SEP
AUG
JUL
JUN
MAY
APR
MAR
FEB
JAN

BERLIN 4 HOURS 674 KG CO_2e

PARIS 6 HOURS 930 KG CO_2e

MÁLAGA 9,5 HOURS 1476 KG CO_2e

TENERIFE 13 HOURS 2106 KG CO_2e

PHUKET 21 HOURS 5264 KG CO_2e

Round-trip from Helsinki

Round-trip emissions for one passenger from Helsinki, Finland, total 10450 kg CO_2e.
SOURCE: ATMOSFAIR.DE

MASTER CLASS IN COOPERATION

Taking the climate challenge can feel lonely if people around you live by other rules. One person's emissions disappear in the big picture. But human are masters of cooperation. In big groups, we have a huge impact—both positive and negative. How can we move from lonely frustration to power in numbers in our climate fight?

People's interactions and patterns of behavior are called **society**. And there's power in numbers. For example, schools are a public service offered by society, and we make decisions related to them together. In contemporary society, many things are built to depend on the overconsumption of fossil fuels and natural resources.

Is the school near the students, or do they need a ride?

Is the school made of concrete or wood? How sustainable is it?

MANY COUNTRIES HAVE COMPULSARY EDUCATION.

THAT'S WHY NEARLY ALL KIDS HAVE TO GO TO SCHOOL.

WE HAVE TO FOLLOW ALL KINDS OF LAWS.

YEAH, THE GOVERNMENT MAKES LOTS OF LAWS.

IMPORTANT LAWS THAT DO THINGS LIKE ABOLISH SLAVERY.

Where does the school's heat and electricity come from?

... AND GIVE WOMEN THE RIGHT TO VOTE!

HOW IS IT POSSIBLE THEY HAD TO PASS LAWS ABOUT THESE THINGS?

THAT'S LIKE, STONE AGE STUFF!

HUMANS ARE CAUSING GLOBAL WARMING— THAT'S PRETTY BACKWARDS, TOO.

WE NEED NEW LAWS FOR THIS!

Society is made up of people—us—and our ways of life. Maybe society will never be perfect. It is **constantly changing** and requires constant modification.

Even though changing a whole society is difficult, it's still **easy** compared to changing the laws of nature. Carbon dioxide, water, and nature as a whole follow natural laws, while society is a human creation and operates according to human requirements.

Next you're going to start counting every time anyone breathes in or out at school to calculate their carbon footprint.

NO, NO! HUMANS ARE PART OF NATURE!

If a lot of food is wasted, the cafeteria's carbon footprint is black as coal. A cafeteria that offers tasty vegetarian food will win the climate race.

What environment is recess held in? Are there trees on the playground? Is it green or asphalt and gravel?

31

STOP READING!

IT'S TOO HARD FOR KIDS!

AND SO BORING!

I DON'T KNOW...

KIDS ARE SMARTER THAN YOU THINK.

Not everyone in the world produces the same emissions. Not everyone consumes the same amount of stuff and natural resources. Who controls the world's emissions? "With great power comes great responsibility," so whose responsibility is it to change the course of climate change?

I WISH I HAD A DOG.

HAVING A PET IS A HUGE REPSONSIBILITY, SINCE OWNERS ARE IN CHARGE OF THEIR PETS' WELL-BEING.

AH, CLASSIC RESPONSIBILITY GIBBERISH.

ADULTS RUIN ALL THE FUN.

THEY HAVE CONTROL OVER HOW MUCH MONEY YOU CAN SPEND AND HOW LATE YOU CAN STAY UP.

SO WHO HAS CONTROL OVER CLIMATE ISSUES?

MAYBE NO ONE WANTS TO TAKE RESPONSIBILITY.

WELL, SINCE THE UNITED STATES IS A DEMOCRACTIC REPUBLIC, MAYBE WE'RE ALL KIND OF RESPONSIBLE?

YOU THINK?

POWER TYPE 1: POLITICS

Not everyone can make decisions about every public issue. So, people choose other people to **decide for them**. Political representatives make laws and decide on taxes. Taxes are used to pay for public services like schools. By adjusting taxes, they can also make something like polluting cheap or expensive.

Because politicians have decision-making power, they have more **responsibility for the consequences** of their decisions than regular citizens. Politicians can steer society towards or away from climate change.

POWER TYPE 2: CELEBRITY

YouTubers, bloggers, vloggers, TV stars, journalists, authors, movie directors... there are all kinds of new and more traditional **opinion leaders** who can make their voices heard in public. Maybe they aren't in politics or fabulously wealthy. But popular celebrities have huge followings.

The power of a celebrity is the attention they get for what they say and do. They bear responsibility for the messages they spread. Celebrities have the opportunity to raise public consciousness about global warming and to show an example of climate-friendly living. Who do you give your **attention** to?

POWER TYPE 3: WEALTH

Some people have accumulated more wealth than others. When you have a lot of money, you can use it for things other than basic necessities like food and heating your home. Money can be used to support research into new forms of energy, buying old growth forests for preservation, or paying influencers to convince other people that the climate isn't really getting warmer. Money brings with it the opportunity to exercise power, and exercising power brings with it a heavy burden of responsibility.

But who is rich? That depends on your frame of reference. Normal everyday Americans are wealthier than most people in the world. Every one of us also consumes more than most of the world's inhabitants, and because of that, we have a greater responsibility for our choices both as individuals and as a nation. Wealth imposes responsibilities on rich people and rich countries and rich companies.

RESPONSIBILITY, PART 2: **THE MONEY GAME**

The international economy encourages people to work together, produces jobs and prosperity (at least for some), and disseminates knowledge. But since goods are produced in all kinds of different places, it can be difficult to see the big picture.

Is business just as honest and fair everywhere? Who is responsible for environmental problems and emissions? In this game, we're making a smartphone, but it could be a car, frozen pizza, or a handbag. The fossil gremlin seems to have his own tips again—can you come up with better instructions for each stage of work?

GRASS ROOTS TO GLOBAL

How can we wake up the world to environmental responsibility? Because every person is a part of society, all behavior also has a social side. The people on this page want to change the world so that the climate won't get warmer and everyone can have a better life. Do they look familiar?

I like being on social media.

I'm only going to spread factual information!

My friends will get interested, too.

THERE IS NO PLANET B

I like designing protest signs.

Enough of us together can show that this is important!

CLIMATE ACTION NOW

FRIDAYS FOR FUTURE

NO INTELLIGENT SPECIES WOULD DESTROY ITS OWN ENVIRONMENT

#CLIMATE REVOLUTION

FRIDAYS FOR FUTURE!

GRETA THUNBERG

Greta was worried about climate change. She started a school strike where she sat on the steps of parliament in Stockholm every Friday. In 2019, countless schoolchildren in thousands of cities around the world spent their Fridays with Greta. Sometimes one person's actions have big results.

I participate in a consumer association.

We raise awareness about the origins of products and tell people about the effects of their choices.

TOTE BAG LOVE

Our company threw out our old way of doing business.

We adopted environmental certifications.

No more greenwashing with false claims.

It makes sense from a business perspective!

CLIMATE STRIKE!

CLIMATE

OUR FUTURE

NONVIOLENT CIVIL DISOBEDIENCE

Mahatma Gandhi wanted to change the status of Indians during a time when the British considered India their property. Gandhi developed a method of nonviolent resistance. One hundred years later, at the end of 2018, the Extinction Rebellion movement began to spread from Britain. Participants in the Extinction Rebellion consider the crisis so urgent and so profound that it has to be brought to everyone's attention, even if it means breaking the law—but always without violence! So, for example, London has had dance parties blocking busy streets, just to make people really stop to think about the issue.

Both protests and civil disobedience are uses of **mass power** that pressure those in power to talk about difficult issues. Raising discussion is a first step that by itself won't stop the climate from getting hotter. Words must lead to action. It's important to find your own way to participate. Some people like being out in front, and they gravitate to leading large groups. Others prefer to be a part of the crowd and enjoy cooperative efforts. One person likes thinking and sharing ideas, and another likes to get their hands dirty and work. Countless people around the world are aiming for **a better tomorrow**.

WHAT IF?

What kind of a world should everyone in the world agree is best? There aren't any easy answers, but it's high time we started using our imaginations. **What if...**

...half of the world was set aside for nature? A mosaic made up of diverse habitats would be protected: land and sea, conifer forests and mangrove swamps, deep ocean corals and prairies. Nature has its own systems for managing change, which also benefit people. Ants, brown algae, and mycelia all play their part in drawing extra carbon out of the atmosphere. Large protected areas make it easier for organisms to adapt to warming, giving plants and animals room to move to areas where they can survive.

...most natural resources are left to nature? Technology would be developed so that a growing population has enough energy for basic necessities. At the same time, we would give up wasting energy and raw materials. Lots of technical solutions exist that are just waiting to be applied. Let's stand side-by-side with decision-makers and companies that make sound decisions even when they squeeze the wallets and behavior of the well-to-do.

... population growth is brought under control? We would ensure access to school all over the world—including for all girls. That may seem like a strange way to prevent global warming, but educated women are the strongest force for restraining population growth. A smaller population would need fewer natural resources.

... a huge change was made to agriculture and forestry? Farming techniques would be selected based on fixing as much carbon as possible in fields while also growing food. Trees would be allowed to play their critical role, being planted and protected for the sake of the stability of the climate and world we know.

But what would we do once half the Earth was set aside for the rest of nature? Would we die of boredom?

41

THE YEAR '89 (1989!)

43

THE YEAR 2020

ERICA AND SVEN WRITE AN EMAIL TO THE WORLD

https://maps.net

San Francisco

The city of San Francisco has ambitious goals to support local nature, public transit, and raw material recycling. What methods do Californian cities have to fight climate change?

Costa Rica

This small Central American country is striving to preserve the diversity of the rain forests and only use renewable energy. What have they achieved there, and how does the future look?

http://emailpost.com

FROM: ericaandsven@mail.com

TO: world@mail.com

SUBJECT: How do we tackle climate change?

Hi!

How's it going? A long, hot summer is coming to an end here, and school has already started. But is there any point going to school if it and everything else might be drowned in a flood in less than a hundred years? Maybe—it depends on what schools teach!

We were thinking that first we need to imagine a better future and then make it happen. We know that you're already seeing climate change where you are, and there's a lot of trouble coming during our lifetimes if we don't act now.

But what do you hope for? What will your home be like in 2050 if we do everything we can to prevent climate change? Then we'll be our parents' age, so super old! :D

Erica and Sven

WHERE IS THE FREON GREMLIN HIDING THESE DAYS?

SEND

Netherlands

...therlands are used to ...th floods, because much ...untry is below sea level. ... of Dutch people have ...eir own government for ...g their feet on climate ...s, because rising sea ...ould endanger the very ...ence of the country.

Ii

Ii, a town of fewer than 10,000 residents in Finland, shows that climate action isn't about size. Maybe in a small area, it's actually easier to get decision-makers, companies, and residents to work together. Children also carry the message as they solve environmental issues in their schools and daycares. They can even tell adults what a life worthy of the future would look like. With decisive action, the people of Ii have significantly reduced their carbon footprint.

India

India is a big country, and there are a lot of Indians. Their emissions are large, too, but in per capita terms, India is a moderate emitter. India has great plans for combating climate change, because desertification, changes to monsoon rains, and floods are real threats to the Indian people. What are they planning there?

Morocco

Morocco sits between the world's largest desert and the Atlantic Ocean. Today, Morocco is one of the only countries that is already making decisions and taking actions aimed at 34.7°F (1.5°C) warming. Will the Moroccan desert become a great source of solar energy?

OH, HIM? HE EXPERIENCED ENLIGHTENMENT, JOINED THE CLIMATE FAIRIES, AND SET OUT TO COLLECT CTC COMPOUNDS FROM THE STRATOSPHERE.

EVERYONE ELSE SEEMS TO BE HAVING FUN.

WHAT DO I DO?

THE GREMLIN REVEALS A POSSIBLE FUTURE

BZZZZ

Greetings from the future!

BLIP

Planet Earth, January 1, 2050

Hey 2021 people!

We imaginary beings can move between the past and the future. Now I'm sending you greetings from 2050. Just think!

Working as a lobbyist was fun for a while, but then I lost my motivation and, for the past few decades, I was just going through the motions. I lost that oil-slick flow. It was time to shift to a greener gear.

I ended up retiring in the late 2020s. Since then, I've been writing my memoirs and hanging out with the family. And I must admit, I enjoy the popularity of my stories. When you've spent decades, centuries even, sowing discord, there are a lot of juicy stories to tell. The best thing is when my readers laugh!

But what should I say about the future? People are so funny when they invent gadgets. If you thought technology was advanced in the twentieth century, just wait for what's coming! We're all done messing around with coal and oil now. We've got a constant flow of energy straight from the Sun. You just have to seize the day and jump on the solar radiation bandwagon.

People finally understand the Earth only has a certain amount of minerals and they have to be recycled—there won't be more once they're gone.

No one admires overconsumption anymore (not even me). There's only one home planet. No one wants to exceed its carrying capacity, but the most frugal people are the true superheroes. Ideas are changing, baby! But people still get rich and fight like they used to, and there are conflicts between countries. We did make a digital leap forward with war, though: national disputes are settled in massive virtual battles. Blood and guts still fly everywhere, but it's all pixels. We came up with this energy solution: The leaders of countries who start the wars have to pedal to create the electricity for the gaming machines. We don't waste solar energy on it! For some reason, all the leaders' negotiation skills have been improving really fast.

In the 2020s, half of the globe was set aside as a playground for nature. They really did it! (Oh, I mean, you really can do it!) There are plenty of people here, more than ever actually. We fit just fine on the planet, though, because most people want to be with family, friends, and even total strangers in cities. But cities have become amazing green oases. All kinds of people and animals are welcome in the future!

Sincerely,
(Ex-fossil) Gremlin

Dear Reader! No one can really send greetings from the future, because it doesn't exist yet.

Building it begins when you imagine it in your mind.

But you are participating in the sequel to the climate story starting now!

LAURA (AUTHOR)

MARI (ILLUSTRATOR)

Sky Pony Press books may be purchased in bulk at special discounts for sales promotion, corporate gifts, fund-raising, or educational purposes. Special editions can also be created to specifications. For details, contact the Special Sales Department, Sky Pony Press, 307 West 36th Street, 11th Floor, New York, NY 10018 or info@skyhorsepublishing.com.

Sky Pony® is a registered trademark of Skyhorse Publishing, Inc.®, a Delaware corporation.

Visit our website at www.skyponypress.com.

10 9 8 7 6 5 4 3 2 1

Manufactured in China, February 2021
This product conforms to CPSIA 2008

Library of Congress Cataloging-in-Publication Data is available on file.

Cover design by Daniel Brount
Cover illustrations by Mari Ahokoivu
Interior design by Maria Mitrunen

Print ISBN: 978-1-5107-6314-2
Ebook ISBN: 978-1-5107-6362-3